FOR MOMMY SO LOVED YOU

WRITTEN BY:
Leigh James

ILLUSTRATED BY:
Embla Granqvist

ISBN-13: 978-7338667-1-2

Book layout by **SelfPublishMe** Consulting and Book Design
Services for Independent Authors. www.selfpublishme.com
email: info@selfpublishme.com

Dedicated to all the single women
brave enough to go it alone.

Once upon a time
Mommy dreamed of you
before you were even born.

You were all Mommy wanted
for a very long time.

Mommy finished school
and bought a house.

She was surrounded by lots of
friends and family, but...

She realized something very important was missing from her life… you!

Because of this
Mommy had a very big hole in her
heart only a special little person
like you could fill.

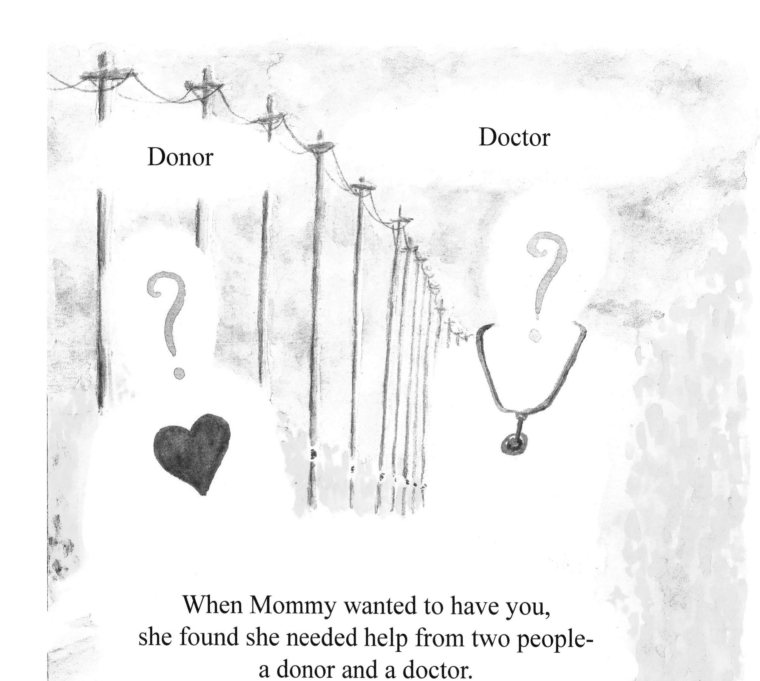

Donor

Doctor

When Mommy wanted to have you,
she found she needed help from two people-
a donor and a doctor.

Mommy searched high and low for the
perfect donor to help create you.

Until one day… Mommy found the donor at a very special bank! You see, this bank didn't hold money, but it held hopes and dreams for those wanting a baby like you.

The bank kept donations from donors who wanted to help someone like Mommy have a baby of their very own one day.

Mommy received a donation
from the Hopes & Dreams Bank
and was very thankful.

Now all Mommy needed
was to find special doctor to help her
with the final step.

Mommy found the special doctor at the clinic!

The doctor worked her magic to combine
the special donation from the donor with
Mommy's egg and you were made!

The doctor put the itsy, bitsy, teeny, tiny you in Mommy's belly so you could grow.

You were held safe and sound in Mommy's belly for a long time... 9 months to be exact.

Over time you grew.
And grew. And grew…
and so did Mommy's belly!

You grew so much that one day
you were too big to fit in Mommy's
belly anymore.

You kicked and kicked
as if to say…

"I WANT OUT!!!"

That was the day Mommy went to the hospital to have you.

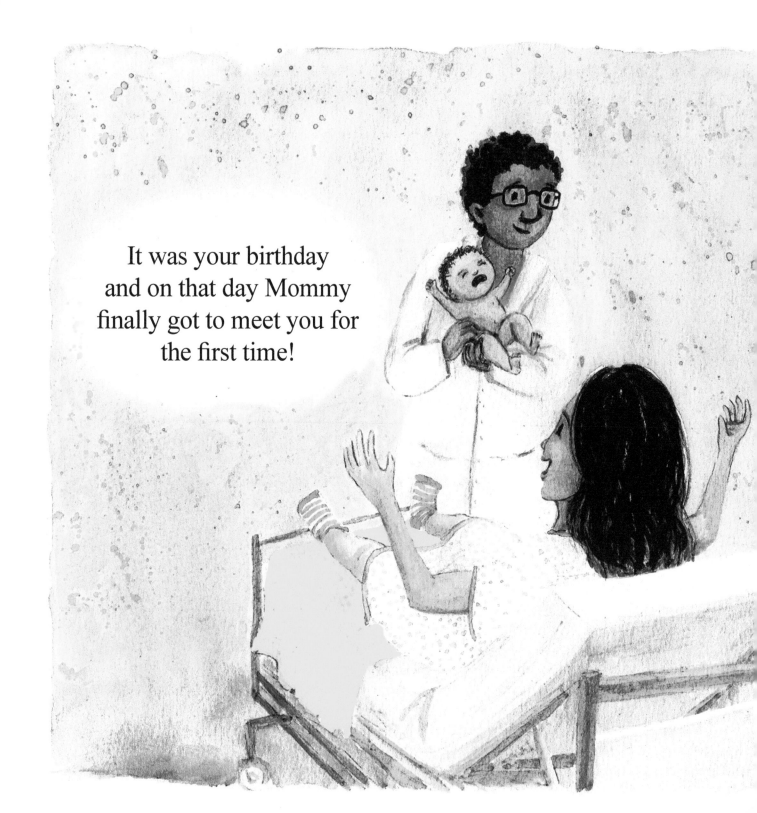

It was your birthday
and on that day Mommy
finally got to meet you for
the first time!

Now Mommy has her baby- *you* to love.

Her heart was filled!

The End

Printed in the USA
CPSIA information can be obtained
at www.ICGtesting.com
LVHW061926221123
764224LV00014B/607